T0368441

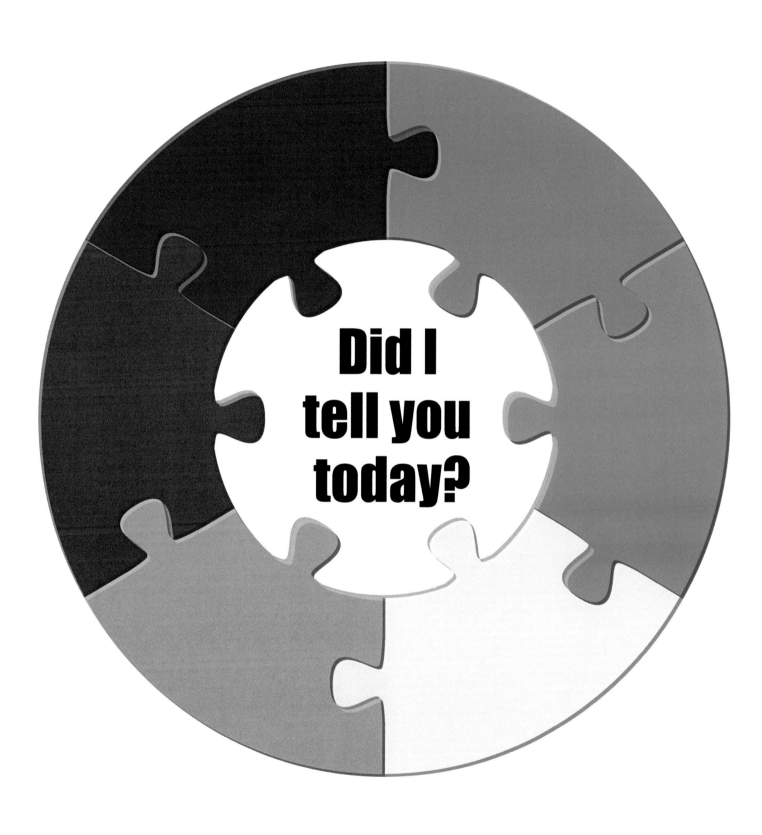

Did I
tell you
today?

Lori Ann Schupbach

Balboa Press books may be ordered through booksellers or by contacting:

Balboa Press
A Division of Hay House
1663 Liberty Drive
Bloomington, IN 47403
www.balboapress.com
844-682-1282

ISBN: 979-8-7652-4169-1 (sc)
ISBN: 979-8-7652-4168-4 (e)

Library of Congress Control Number: 2023914083

Print information available on the last page.

Balboa Press rev. date: 11/03/2023

BALBOA.PRESS
A DIVISION OF HAY HOUSE

Dedication page

To my son Jesse,
You are Inspiring!
May the purpose of your life touch many in profound
and meaningful ways, and may
You feel Impactful!

Introduction — Engage now

The development of the concepts and application of this book comes from a new mother's intuition sparked by the inspiration that only a new child could bring to the world. Moving years ahead, science has made revolutionary strides in shedding light on the power and development of the mind of your baby and very young child.

These applications will facilitate a profound relationship between you and your child; most importantly, your child will develop a strong, secure, and meaningful relationship with him or herself.

As you will learn, there is an extraordinary window of opportunity to imprint your child's core with essential truths; that we as adults can now only dream that this could have been done for us. Your child will spend the rest of his or her life building on this solid foundation that you help set down.

These applications will be of tremendous benefit to your child and you will find that by using these particular words and concepts with your child, you too will directly benefit as you say, repeat, and experience these words with them.

There was a day in 2009 when my intuition lead me to speak to my newborn son, now fourteen years old, in a peculiar and particular way. I looked at him and said, "Oh, did I tell you who you are today?" And the affirmations over his life began to roll out of my mouth. He did not know what I was saying at the time, but he did like it and responded with coos and smiles to the connection and fluctuations. Over the past thirteen years, the science behind the formative years of our minds, the words we use, and the need for positive reinforcement through learning, engaging, love, and socializing has expanded. More than ever, we need to grow our parental toolbox to build the next generation of little beings to be strong, capable, and ready for life.

"The greatest good you can do for another is not just to share your riches, but to reveal to him his own."

—Benjamin Disraeli

As a new parent, you have just started the most important journey you will ever take. You are now responsible not only for yourself but also for the cultivation of another soul's journey. This is the highest honor and privilege one can have. You have just embarked on a world full of possibilities. You have a chance to create and be creative. This is a time to build and, most importantly, a time to share love, the kind of love that will create a meaningful and profound effect on the life of your child.

- **You are** the architect, building a strong, solid foundation for your little one
- **You are** the artist, with a magnificent, unique canvas
- **You are** the teacher at the school of the good life
- **You are** the biochemist who now has the most powerful codes
- **You are** the number one most important person to your child
- **You are** the source of love for the new soul you are responsible for
- **You feel** empowered with the keys to your child's best life

Just as we have as adults, our children will define themselves by what they hear, what they see, how they feel, and what they experience through their senses. As they grow and develop, they will gather this information from the foundational internal memory bank that we create for them to draw from. What we say, how we make them feel, and the experiences we create for them will be the building block of their identity. Once the foundation has been laid, as children grow, they will depend on this early but powerful and foundational information to move forward as the co-creator of their awe-inspired destiny.

"Our experiences with the outside world are determined by what is established in our inner world."

—Lori Ann Schupbach

We want to give our children the very best edge in life.

We want them to be happy, fulfilled, whole, and responsible; have meaningful friendships; make good decisions; and love themselves and the world they live in.

We see our children having a clean slate to be, do, and have it all.

We hope that their life is better than we can imagine.

As adults, we try to make sense of it all—the choices we have made and the moments that have defined us, both fortunate and unfortunate. We try to find the reasons for why we do what we do and think what we think.

What were the driving factors in ourselves that lead us to this very moment? What could have given us an advantage that we did not otherwise have? How can we give our children advantages to help them avoid becoming adults that need fixing?

"The self-help industry was valued at $10 billion in 2019 and is projected to reach $13.2 billion by 2023. The Compound Annual Growth Rate (CAGR) of the self-improvement market is projected at 5.1% from 2020 to 2027." This is a clear sign that we have gotten off the path of knowing who we are; we have been derailed from remembering the authentic and perfect human beings we were born to be. We have been too easily influenced by life's circumstances.

The weather of life experiences can tear a house down if it does not have a strong foundation. The foundation of the human soul is understood in many philosophies as being the innermost aspect of the human being, which gives meaning and purpose to life. It is considered to be the foundation of human consciousness, self-awareness, and the ability to reflect and make choices. The quality of our soul influences the mind, and the mind stores information acquired through repetition, reflecting our beliefs, memories, and life experiences. The subconscious is the part of the mind that is responsible for many of our automatic behaviors and reactions, such as breathing and digestion, and for storing and processing memories, emotions, and other information not immediately available to our conscious awareness. This information stored in our subconscious directly affects our behavior and actions in every situation, even into adulthood. It is now your honor to build a foundation for your children that will make them strong, resilient, and full of self-love and acceptance, giving them the edge we all spend our lives striving for.

"It is easier to build strong children than to repair broken adults."

—F. Douglas

The Science — Overlooked Physiological Development of the Baby Brain

What the science tells us about your baby's brain development and where the greatest effects comes from is nothing less than remarkable; it can empower you to greatly influence your children for the rest of their lives.

"New research from the University of Maryland and Harvard University suggests that young infants benefit from hearing words repeated by their parents. With this knowledge, parents may make conscious communication choices that could pay off in their babies' toddler years and beyond."

A lot of recent focus has been on simply talking more to your child -- but how you talk to your child matters. It isn't just about the number of words.

"They found that the toddlers with stronger language outcomes differed in two ways from their peers: their parents had repeated words more often, and they were more tuned into the language as infants. The findings from this study will perhaps encourage parents to be more conscious of repeating words to maximize language development benefits."

"It is the quality of the input that matters most, not just the quantity," said Dr. Rowe.

Harvard University- "Brain Architecture in Infants"

Early experiences affect the development of brain architecture, which provides the foundation for all future learning, behavior, and health. Just as a weak foundation compromises the quality and strength of a house, adverse experiences early in life can impair brain architecture, with negative effects lasting into adulthood.

The basic architecture of the brain is constructed through an ongoing process that begins before birth and continues into adulthood.

The early years are the most active period for establishing neural connections...

Neural connections and skills form first, followed by more complex circuits and skills. In the first few years of life, more than 1 million new neural connections form every second.

The connections that form early provide either a strong or a weak foundation for the connections that form later.

Center of the developing child– Harvard University

"The science of early brain development can inform investments in early childhood. These basic concepts, established over decades of neuroscience and behavioral research, help illustrate why child development—particularly from birth to five years—is a foundation for a prosperous and sustainable society."

"The most important period of life is not the age of university studies, but the first one, the period from birth to the age of six."

—Maria Montessori

What Is Happening on the Inside?

Bruce H. Lipton, PhD, on the relevancy of the subconscious mind

"The most influential perceptual programming of the subconscious mind occurs from birth through age six. It is important to realize that perceptions acquired before the age of six become the fundamental subconscious programs that shape the character of an individual's life.

During this time of accelerated learning, Nature facilitates the enculturation process by developmentally enhancing the subconscious mind's ability to download massive amounts of information. We know this thanks to our study of brainwaves in adults and children.

Electroencephalogram EEG vibrations continuously shift from state to state over the whole range of frequencies during normal brain processing in adults. However, brain frequencies in developing children display radically different behavior. EEG vibration rates and their corresponding states evolve in incremental stages over time.

The predominant brain activity during the child's first two years of life is delta, the lowest EEG frequency range. Between two and six years of age, the child's brain activity ramps up and operates primarily in the range of theta. While in the theta state, children spend much of their time mixing the imaginary world with the real world.

The predominant delta and theta activity expressed by children younger than six signifies that their brains are operating at levels below consciousness. Delta and theta brain frequencies define a brain state known as a hypnagogic trance—the same neural state that hypnotherapists use to directly download new behaviors into the subconscious minds of their clients.

In other words, the first six years of a child's life are spent in a hypnotic trance!

A child's perceptions of the world are directly downloaded into the subconscious during this time, without discrimination and without filters of the analytical self-conscious mind, which does not fully exist.

Consequently, our fundamental perceptions about life and our role in it are learned without our having the capacity to choose or reject those beliefs. We were simply programmed.

Once programmed, that information would inevitably influence 95 percent of that individual's behavior for the rest of his or her life."

"We see how early childhood experiences are so important to lifelong outcomes, how the early environment literally becomes embedded in and changes its architecture."

—Andrew S. Garner

The Spirit—Missed Essentials

What is spirit? And are we born with one? I think it is important to take a look at the whole picture of what makes us who we are. We are well aware of our physical existence; in fact, it is the driving factor of our lives. However, what about the aspects of us we don't give our attention to? Our breath, the very intricate workings of our body that allows us animation. The whole body system that works without our knowledge or instruction. We must get to a place where we are able to consider beyond what we touch, taste, and see if we want to get beyond our limiting systems.

It is important to consider the original context and meaning of the words we use. When we look at the root of the language down to its original form—in this case, considering Greek and Hebrew—we find that there is a depth that provides a greater understanding of these words. In this case, we will take a short dive into the word *spirit* so we can unveil any missed essentials and avoid keeping ourselves in ignorance of the whole person.

First, let us start with what is common to us as we search for clear meaning. Then we will progress a bit to make sure we do not miss any essentials of truth.

Webster's Dictionary tells us that *spirit* is a noun (person, place, or thing) with the following definition "the immaterial intelligent or sentient part of a person."

The *Oxford English Dictionary* defines *spirit* as "the part of a person that includes their mind, feeling, and character rather than their body."

It is vital that we bring the Bible into the discussion because it brings a deeper understanding of what our modern language and understanding tell us about spirit. Since we agree that words are important, let us get the most out of every word that comes out of our mouths.

The Bible tells us the following:

"And be renewed in the spirit of your mind" (Ephesians 4:23, KJV).

"The grace of our Lord Jesus Christ be with your spirit. Amen" (Philemon 1:25, KJV).

If we look at the originating language in *Strong's Concordance* or in a Bible dictionary of Hebrew and Greek, we gain a deeper understanding to our modern language of the word *spirit*.

Hebrew= נְשָׁמָה neshâmâh, nesh-aw-maw'; from H5395; a puff, i.e. wind, angry or *vital breath, divine inspiration, intellect.* or (concretely) an animal:—blast, (that) breath(-eth), *inspiration, soul, spirit.*

Greek= πνεῦμα pneûma, pnyoo'-mah; from G4154; a current of air, i.e. *breath* (blast) or a breeze; by analogy or figuratively, a spirit, i.e. (human) the rational soul, (by implication) *vital principle, mental disposition.*

The applications for the purposes of this book are brief and meant as an introduction to looking into words as we contemplate the spirit of what we want to instill in our children. The multiple and various studies of this subject and the Bible are extensive and can lead down a fascinating path of truth and life. The point of exploring this subject is to take the illusiveness or intimidation out of the concept of spirit. We all have one, and it needs some attention and consideration. You and your child have a spirit.

To sum it up, we see that we have a spirit defined as an "immaterial intelligent or sentient part" (*Webster's*) and "the part of a person that includes our minds, feeling, and character rather than our bodies" (*Oxford*). We see that we have "vital breath and intellect" (Hebrew), and lastly we see that we have "a vital principle, mental disposition" (Greek).

So we see that spirit has to do with a few factors of our communication, our breath, our minds, our feelings, and our intellect.

My hope is that you feel empowered with knowledge and understanding of why it is imperative to communicate with your children in a way that strengthens their minds, bodies, souls, and spirits.

"For just as the body without the spirit is dead, so faith without actions is also dead."

—*James 2:26, International Standard Version*

The Power—Misunderstood Fundamentals of Expression

"Words have power. Their meaning crystallizes perceptions that shape our beliefs, drive our behavior, and ultimately create our world. Their power arises from our emotional responses when we read, speak, or hear them."

"The more we hear, read, or speak a word or phrase, the more power it has over us. This is because the brain uses repetition to learn, searching for patterns and consistency as a way to make sense of the world around us."

This book will give you the power and control to build a solid foundation for your new baby and young child. It will support you in cultivating a simple yet profound bonding time. It will encourage your creativity in how you speak with love, excitement, and in fluctuation to your child. The more you put your own spin on how you read this book to encourage a deep sense of feeling for your little one, the deeper the roots of what you are planting will be.

Words can completely change a life. Yes, words are important because we need them to communicate, but the way that words are presented, spoken, and written is a whole different level of communication. I encourage you to use this book creatively, putting your own spin on how you speak the words and talk about the pictures, letters, numbers, and colors to your child. The more you attach feelings to the words, the more profound the long-term effects will be. This book will help you consciously harness the power of words for your child's benefit for the rest of his or her life.

"It's way too early for him to be talking anyhow but I see in his eyes something and I see in his eyes a voice and I see in his eyes a whole new set of words."

—Sherman Alexie

Colors, Shapes, Numbers, and Letters

This book will grow with your child's abilities from birth to five years of age.

Color—From birth to three months, your baby will see the monochrome use of gray, black, and white.

By three months of age, experts say most babies can see color, with a preference for bright primary colors for brain stimulation.

Around the age of six to eight months, a baby's color vision is well developed.

By teaching your child about color, you will also be helping them to use color as a means of **creative expression** in all aspects of life.

In color therapy, we see that colors are associated with feelings.

Red: vitality, self-confidence, safety
Orange: happiness, increased social confidence, joy
Yellow: cheerfulness, mental clarity, confidence
Green: peace, love, harmony, relaxation
Blue: communication, confidence in speaking
Purple: creativity, inspiration, generosity

Shapes—Shapes are building blocks for several bigger concepts.

Same and *different* are the basics of **observational skills.**

Categorization is the detailed recognition of objects.

Problem-solving and trait recognition is key for future science skills.

Numbers—The more we talk numbers, the better chance infants and toddlers have to build **a positive attitude toward math learning and learning in general.**

Letters—Research shows that from the early age of three months, babies can learn languages. The alphabet is the **foundation of language**.

"Babies are thinking and attracting before they are speaking. Even though you are only months old in your physical body, you are a very old and wise Creator, focused on that baby's body."

—Abraham Hicks

Instructions—Read the Book Like This

You Are Awe-Inspiring
You Feel Amazing

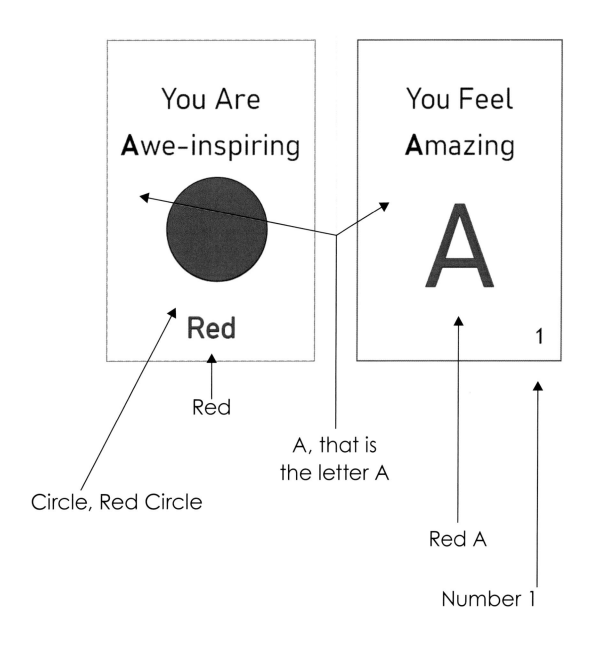

Incorporate expressive interjections and vocal variety with fluctuations by adding words that provide sound and emotion.

- **OOOhh ...** Did I tell you today?

- **Ahhh ...** You Are Awe-Inspiring

- **Oh yes ...** You Feel Amazing

- **Aha ...** Look, a circle—a red circle

- **Whoa ...** the letter A

- **Wow ...** it's red

- **Yay ...** the number one

Varying your pitch to maintain your child's attention and evoke a response.

- Change your pitch from low to high **=** surprise, suspense

- Change your pitch from high to low **=** confidence, finality

- Use high and low pitch within the same word **=** power, certainty

- Whisper **=** comforting, bonding, intimate

- Use your own unique melody (rhythm and pitch) together as you navigate the points on the page **=** evoke feelings of happiness

When you are reading aloud to your baby in a way that engages him or her, it helps improve his or her emerging literacy and language development. In addition, strengthen the bond between baby and parent. Make sure to take the time to notice your child's reactions and enjoy yourself!

"The way we talk to our children becomes their inner voice."

— Peggy O'Mara

References

University, Harvard. "InBrief: The Science of Early Childhood Development." Center on the Developing Child at Harvard University, October 29, 2020. http://developingchild.harvard.edu/resources/inbrief-science-of-ecd/.

Sadeghi, Habib. "The Power of Words: How Words Affect Our Lives | Goop." Goop, May 29, 2014. https://goop.com/wellness/mindfulness/the-scary-power-of-negative-words/.

University of Maryland. "Benefits of word repetition to infants: Repeat after me! Parents who repeat words to 7-month-olds have toddlers with larger vocabularies." ScienceDaily. www.sciencedaily.com/releases/2015/09/150921103539.htm (accessed July 20, 2023).

Marketdata, Gitnux. "The Latest Self-Help Industry Statistics 2023 You Shouldn't Ignore • GITNUX." blog.gitnux.com, March 23, 2023. https://blog.gitnux.com/self-help-industry-statistics/.

University, Harvard. "Brain Architecture." Center on the Developing Child at Harvard University, August 20, 2019. http://developingchild.harvard.edu/science/key-concepts/brain-architecture/.

College of behavioral social sciences. "Repeating Words to Infants Boosts Language Development | BSOS | Behavioral & Social Sciences College | University of Maryland." Umd.edu, 2021. https://bsos.umd.edu/featured-content/repeating-words-infants-boosts.

Lipton, Bruce H Ph.D. "Are You Programmed at Birth?" www.healyourlife.com, August 17, 2010. https://www.healyourlife.com/are-you-programmed-at-birth.

You Are
Awe-inspiring

RED

You Feel **A**mazing

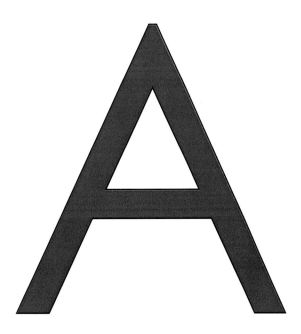

You Are
Brave

ORANGE

You Feel
Bold

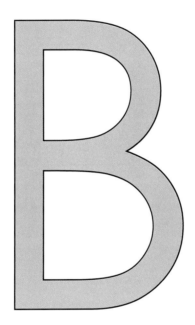

You Are
Creative

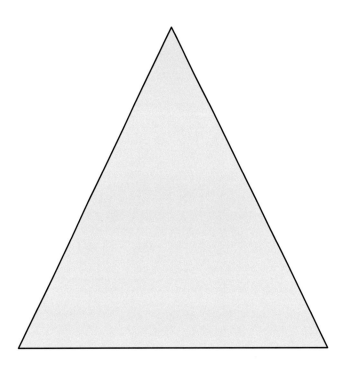

YELLOW

You Feel
Clever

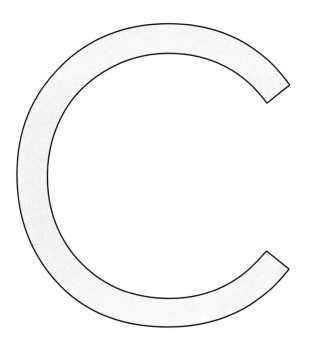

You Are
Determined

GREEN

You Feel
Discovered

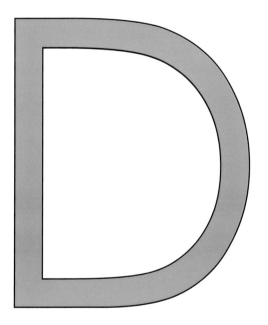

You Are
Empowered

BLUE

You Feel
Encouraged

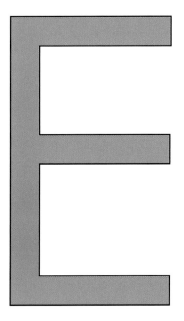

You Are
Faithful

PURPLE

You Feel
Fortunate

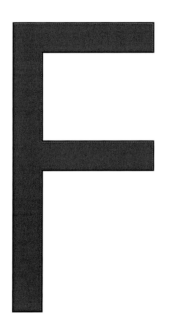

6

You Are
Grateful

GRAY

You Feel
Generous

7

You Are
Honest

PINK

You Feel
Humble

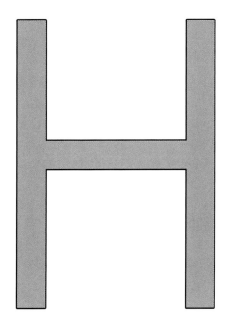

8

You Are

Interesting

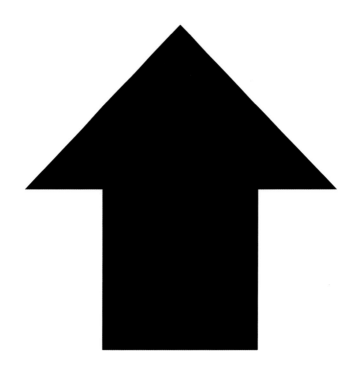

BLACK

You Feel **I**mportant

You Are
Joyful

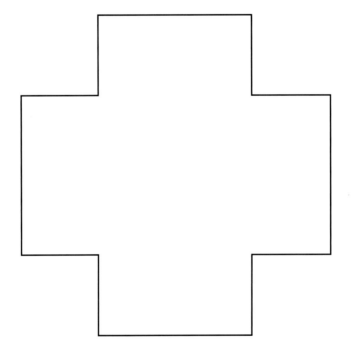

WHITE

You Feel
Jolly

You Are
Kindhearted

RED

You Feel
Kind

K

11

You Are
Lovable

ORANGE

You Feel
Loved

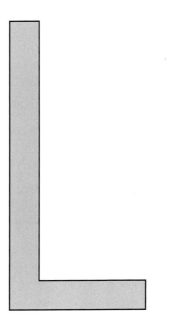

You Are
Motivated

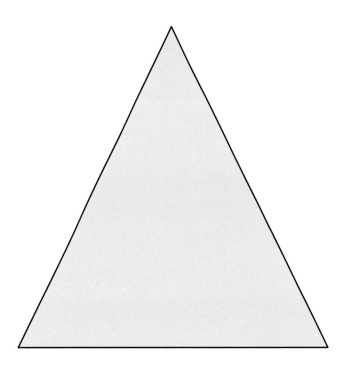

YELLOW

You Feel
Meaningful

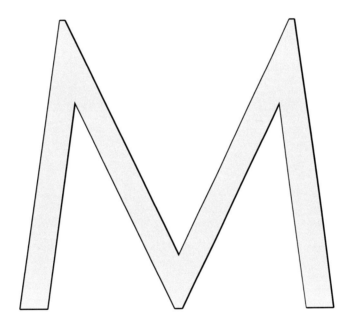

13

You Are
Noble

GREEN

You Feel **N**urtured

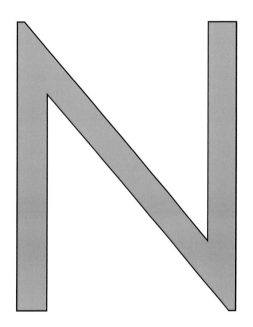

14

You Are
Original

BLUE

You Feel
Optimistic

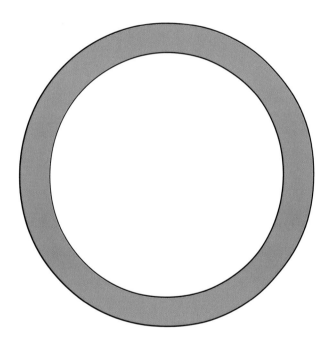

15

You Are
Peaceful

PURPLE

You Feel
Patient

P

16

You Are
Quality

GRAY

You Feel **Q**ualified

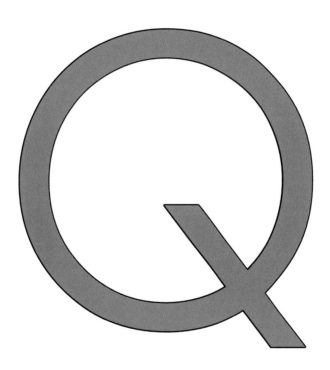

17

You Are
Respectful

PINK

You Feel
Responsible

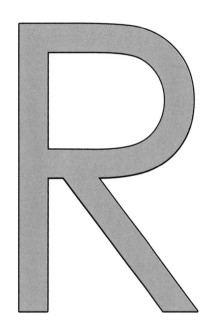

18

You Are Special

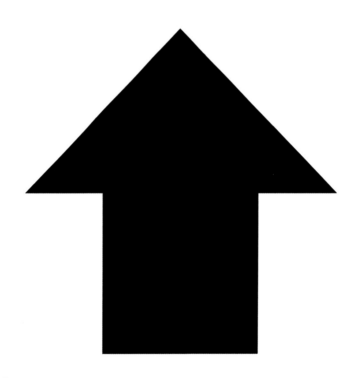

BLACK

You Feel Supported

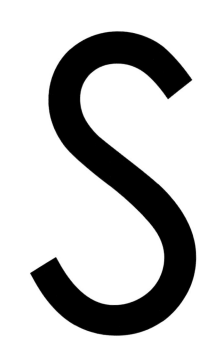

You Are Talented

WHITE

You Feel **T**hankful

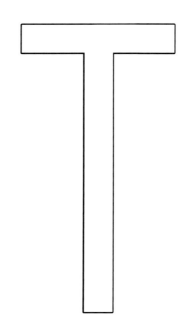

You Are
Unique

RED

You Feel
Useful

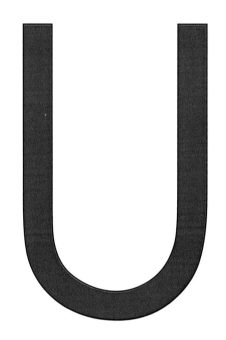

21

You Are
Valued

ORANGE

You Feel
Vibrant

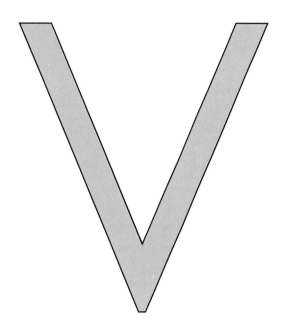

22

You Are
Wise

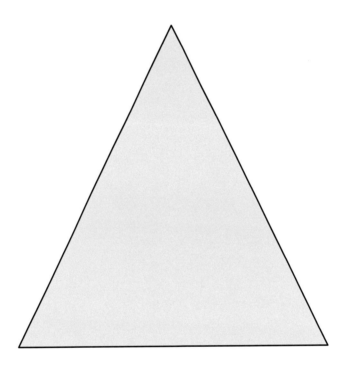

YELLOW

You Feel **W**onderful

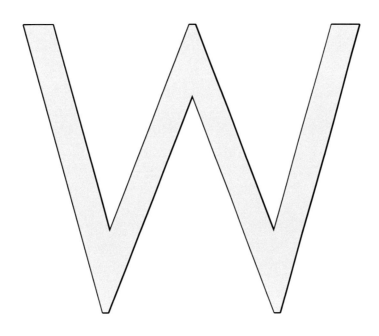

You Are eXtraordinary

GREEN

You Feel EXcellent

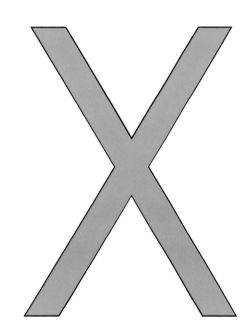

You Are

Yourself

BLUE

You Feel **Y**outhful

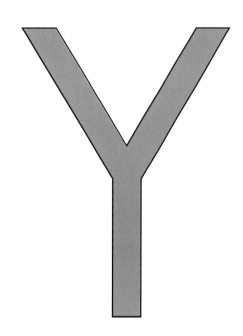

You Are
Zealous

PURPLE

You Feel
Zany

Z

26

Printed in the United States
by Baker & Taylor Publisher Services